JOY FILLED MARRIAGE

Mindful habits to become a better wife and live in peace with your husband.

HELEN LORI

COPYRIGHT

Copyright © 2021 by HELEN LORI: All rights reserved. This book or any portion thereof may not be reproduced or used in any manner whatsoever without the express written permission of the author except for the use of brief quotations in a book review.

TABLE OF CONTENTS

INTRODUCTION

Respect between spouses is essential for a successful and fulfilled relationship in marriage. Investing in your marriage by taking care of your husband is critical to both his and your health. In the midst of life's chaos, nourishing him can easily fall by the wayside. As his wife, you must establish regular practices that not only keep you linked, but also enhance your bond.

Men and women have been designed differently when it comes to our basic needs. There are several things that guys seek in a relationship but will never tell you about, one of which is respect. Rather than debating his points of view or engaging in an argument or even a brawl over something trivial, show him that you trust him. You're charging your husband's batteries when you show him how much you admire and respect what he does or thinks. He'll be ready to fight the world knowing he has you by his side.

Never make an irrational remark about your partner. In a marriage, men and women are absolutely equal; nonetheless, we are born with different sets of needs. A husband and wife can meet each other's needs through marriage. This book is an excellent resource for helping to establish a stronger and better partnership, regardless of the obstacles that may emerge. Now is the time to demonstrate your sincere love for your husband via actions.

CHAPTER 1
Caring for Your Husband

You adore your husband as a good wife, but there is a difference between showing love and acting in love. It's not just about saying, "I love you." Now is the time to get down to business. In this chapter, I would be sharing some ideas for you to show your husband that you truly care. While assumptions about what men and women should do exist, you should not allow them dictate how you act in your relationship. Instead, try to strike a balance that is beneficial to both of you. If you're strong at balancing the books and he's good at organizing the desk, you should focus on your strengths. The most essential thing is to find the right balance for your relationship. Even if you don't think your husband is always courteous to you, make sure he understands that he is your number one priority. Don't make fun of him in front of his friends or family. Even if you disagree, always be respectful of how he feels about something. Even if you don't say it to his face all of the time, make sure he knows you respect him. Men like to be appreciated, and a lot of their sadness and rage stems from the sensation that they are being disrespected by others. If you care about each other, it's natural for you to want to make each other happy. Listed below are some great tips to show your husband you truly care about him each day.

Love Him in His Own Language: Showing your husband love in the language he prefers is a wonderful approach to show him you care. It won't always come naturally to love from his point of view, but when it does, he'll know you're paying attention to him and his specific needs. When does your husband seem to take pleasure in your affection? Focus on those areas and bless him, whether it's acts of service, loving words, gifts, shared activities, or any other display of love. He'll appreciate your efforts to make him feel special.

Affirm Him: Bathing your husband in affirmation is one of the most crucial things you can do for him. Adding supportive words to your interactions will help you create a deeper degree of connection in your marriage. Give your husband words that make him feel special, appreciated, and treasured. Commend him on his abilities, charity, or work ethic. Tell him which of his characteristics are gifts to you and others. Build him up on a daily basis by consistently filling his cup. Asking your husband for advice, his opinion, or to share his knowledge demonstrates that you acknowledge and value his abilities and contributions. It naturally incorporates him into your couple's choices and decisions. In the long term, being liberal with your praise will pay off handsomely. Keep in mind that your husband will be able to determine whether or not the words you say to him are genuine.

Flirt with Him: Flirting with your husband is a terrific method to show him that you care about him and that you like him. It's most likely one of the characteristics that attracted him to you when you were dating. Flirt with him using your words, body language, and the power of touch. Every day, make a conscious effort to touch him softly. Words are one thing, but touch is a whole other ballgame. Touch imprints itself on our memory, amplifying our shared experiences. This isn't necessarily the kind of physical contact that leads to sex; rather, it's the kind of touch that keeps the two of you connected outside of intimacy. It's never too late to start flirting with your husband again if you haven't done so in a while. He'll appreciate your rekindled adoration and will most likely reciprocate it.

Allow Him to Be Who He Is: In the early stages of a relationship, we sometimes fail to notice each other's peculiarities or habits, which might be irritating or difficult to bear. We see such things more clearly as we settle into a long-term relationship. Once you've figured out your husband's personality traits, it can be tempting to want to change him. Instead, let go of the desire to transform him. Those eccentricities that irritate you can end up endearing you to him. You married your husband because of who he is. Allow him to be that person, and you'll both benefit. These behaviors will benefit you both as you navigate life together. Pay close attention to your husband to figure out what he requires to be his best self. Raise him up; be a safe haven for him, a constant source of love and encouragement.

Make Yourself Available To Him: Make yourself available to your husband in every manner you can. Make yourself available. Be his best friend, confidante, and lover. He's counting on you! Give him your time generously, meeting his wants with love. It's vital to be sexually available to your husband, but it can be difficult for busy wives. Make sure you give yourself time to emotionally and physically prepare for intimacy. He will appreciate your efforts, and the two of you will profit much. Spending time with him in his element, sharing activities that are meaningful to him could also be very meaningful to him. Even if his favourite pastimes aren't your cup of tea, if you choose to participate with him in them regardless, he'll notice and appreciate it.

CHAPTER 2
How to rekindle Passion in Your Marriage

When you gaze into your partner's eyes, you will see passion. We may do this by using our eyes, body language, prioritizing unhurried time with each other, affirming, complimenting, and building up our partner in ways that make them proud to be a man or a woman. It's also about paying attention to ourselves and nourishing our senses, allowing desire to organically develop and flow, respecting our inner selves, and presenting ourselves in ways that make us feel distinct, sophisticated, fun, and sexy. It's about being totally there for your partner on a regular basis in proactive, sensory-rich ways.

Most of us have contemplated or tried various methods for rekindling love in a relationship. Some romantic ties are simply worth a second chance. Knowing how to reignite love in a relationship certainly doesn't harm when you're serious about doing so successfully. Emotional intimacy and closeness are the foundations of a good sexual relationship. To put it another way, if you want to improve your physical relationship, you must first strengthen your emotional relationship. Concentrate on addressing your partner's demands while also articulating your own in a caring and polite manner. Don't get caught up in a cycle where you demand certain things from each other, such as respect and kindness, but are hesitant to be the first to provide it to them. Always keep in mind that fortune favours the bold. The hazards of love are that much more severe and frightening, which is why love is regarded such a delicious reward.

Complement each other's masculinity or femininity: Wives, say anything that makes your man feel like a man, such as, "I admire the way you led the meeting the other day." "You're a fantastic lover. That was incredible. Men may make their wife happy and feel like the most beautiful woman in the room by assisting her in feeling confident. She is a lady! Your beauty takes my breath away even when you're only standing near the window in the sunlight, I admire how gentle you are with our children.

Gentle touch: When helping your wife through a door, place your hand over her hand while driving, or delicately raise her hand to your lips and kiss it. While he's driving, gently rub the back of his neck, or rest your head on his shoulder while watching TV.

Make some wiggle time: If at all possible, keep a chunk of your weekends free to allow for at least a half-day of unscheduled time with your partner. If time is limited after work, have a regular happy hour or half-hour sitting together on the porch in the summer, cuddling up on a couch, or soaking in a bubble bath.

Pretend it's a first date: Meet in the middle of the day at a coffee shop or café, or get together after work for a glass of wine, and pretend to be two individuals deeply attracted to each other.

Read an interesting Book: Reading may provide inspiration. Read anything that makes you think about things differently and makes you ask yourself new questions. When the timing is appropriate, whether out for a walk or sitting on the front porch before supper, express some of the ideas you've been thinking about, seek her opinion, and listen to her response. Demonstrate that you value her thoughts and opinions.

Value your inner beauty as a woman: Believe that you have a unique beauty that no one else has, and never let go of this aspect of yourself. The assurance that comes from a woman who values the beauty that God has given her will be irresistible.

Laugh together: Laughter is one of the most underappreciated aphrodisiacs in the world. Watch some funny movies or cartoons, or share an amusing YouTube video with your partner. Never be hesitant to tell a nice tale about yourself, as discussing our shortcomings with our soul mate is a powerful method of connecting.

Be Responsive: Make an effort to be more open with your emotions, particularly the good and tender ones. Don't keep your feelings of thanks for the beauty of the day, your wife's affection, or your children's cuteness to yourself. Declare it. Say it with vigour and conviction.

Show Gratitude: You'll be surprised at how these two tiny words, when said generously, may enhance the love and romantic link. Try this: praise the one you love for at least one thing they did, or one thing they are, that brightens your life every evening, between dinner and lights-out, when you are together.

CHAPTER 3

Healthy and Tasty Desserts FOR YOUR HUBBY

Men and women have equal dietary requirements, but they do not have the same eating habits. The average American guy consumes roughly 2,700 calories per day, 500 more than he needs and 650 more than the average woman, with far more of that food being pure junk: Guys consume nearly double the recommended amount of salt, and their diets are often deficient in vitamins A, D, and E. Men also consume only around half of the recommended daily fiber intake of 38 grams. You may tackle this problem by making a healthy dinner every night and packing him a well-thought-out lunch box every morning. But chances are you're not only working as many hours as he does, but you're also shouldering greater responsibility at home. However, you can encourage your partner to consume more of specific foods to ensure that he is happier and healthier, or at the very least stays around long enough to pay off the mortgage. Foods that have been proved to be particularly beneficial at flattening the male belly and turbocharging the little guy in the center have been identified. If you don't get a marital upgrade after leaving more of these meals in the fridge, consider sharing the great new site for males, Best Life, with him. He'll learn about foods that will keep him young forever, as well as style and love advice.

Fruits and vegetables are healthy and help to keep you full so you don't get hungry. Filling your plate with fruits and vegetables will likely eliminate the need for vitamin supplements, reduce hunger, and train your taste buds to prefer fewer sweet and salty foods. Try using enticing terms to describe veggies to urge your family to eat them. Instead of just saying green beans, try something more intriguing like sweet, sizzling green beans with crisp almonds. Mealtimes should be scheduled on a regular basis. If everyone in the family eats at the same time and snacks are only available when meals are spaced apart, you'll be astonished at how much weight loss occurs. People who eat at regular intervals are less likely to overeat. It's difficult to quit eating once you start, so limit yourself to three meals and one snack per day. Starting the day with a nutritious meal is critical to performing at your best throughout the day. Cereal with yogurt or milk, as well as fruit juice or fruit, are ideal for a simple and nutritious breakfast.

Tomato sauce: Men who consume more than 10 servings of tomatoes each week have an 18% decreased risk of acquiring prostate cancer. Garden vegetables may also help to keep your man healthy and glowing.

Spinach: Leafy and green spinach is high in magnesium, a mineral that reduces inflammation in blood vessels and hence improves blood flow. When it comes to a man's health, blood flow is crucial. Increased blood flow to the extremities increases arousal and makes sex more enjoyable, similar to Viagra. Spinach is also high in folate, which helps to protect your guy from age-related sexual difficulties by increasing blood flow to the nether regions.

Watermelon: This amazing fruit watermelon is one of the best natural sources of L-citrulline, an amino acid that can help your husband achieve a stronger erection. It turns to L-arginine in the body, which stimulates the creation of nitric oxide, which improves blood flow to the penis and strengthens erections.

Coffee: Men who eat two to three cups of coffee per day, or 85 to 170 milligrams of caffeine from other beverages, are 42 percent less likely to suffer from erectile dysfunction than those who consume less caffeine. The pattern holds true for males who are overweight, obese, or hypertensive, but not for those who have diabetes, which is a common source of the problem. This stimulant causes a chain of events in the body, culminating in increased blood flow to the penis.

Green Tea: This calm and detoxify your man. Green tea contains catechins, which have been found to burn belly fat and increase the liver's ability to convert fat into energy.

Red wine: Tasty and colourful red wine's high antioxidant content also stimulates the creation of nitric oxide, which relaxes arterial walls. This increases blood flow to the lower body, causing sensations of sexual arousal. Red wine is especially high in the heart-healthy resveratrol, which will assist your love's heart stay in peak shape.

Pesto: This is another great source of nourishment for your husband. Pesto is high in zinc, thanks to the pine nuts that make up its basis. Men who have higher levels in their system have higher sex desires than men who have lower levels. Pine nuts are also high in magnesium, which helps to increase testosterone and maintain sperm healthy and viable.

Brazil nuts: Selenium, a trace mineral contained in Brazil nuts, is essential for hormone function. Although just a little amount is required for healthy sperm, even a minor shortage can be fatal to reproductive health.

Tuna: It's no secret that omega-3 fatty acids abound in oily Coldwater fish like wild salmon, sardines, and tuna, but here's something you might not know: Not only does this mineral help your heart, but it also boosts dopamine levels in your brain. Dopamine makes you feel more at ease and connected to your partner, making sex more enjoyable.

Honey: Unlike table sugar, honey contains healthy chemicals such as quercetin, which has been demonstrated to improve athletic endurance and prevent depression. Honey also has a less dramatic effect on blood sugar levels than ordinary sugar, so it won't cause his body to go into fat-storage mode like the white stuff.

Broccoli: As men get older, their estrogen levels rise while their testosterone levels decrease. Indoles, which are anti-cancer chemicals, can help achieve a balance. Indoles are found in cruciferous vegetables like broccoli, and they help stimulate testosterone levels by breaking down and eliminating excess estrogen from the body, which suppresses the development of male sex hormones.

Pumpkin Seeds: This is good for your husband as pumpkin seeds are one of the best sources of zinc and magnesium in the diet. Essential minerals have been demonstrated to increase testosterone and growth hormone levels, especially when taken together. In fact, one eight-week study found that college football players who took a nightly zinc-magnesium supplement had a 30 percent boost in testosterone levels and a 13 to 16 percent improvement in leg strength. The seeds are also high in polyunsaturated fatty acids, which have been shown to increase prostaglandins, hormone-like compounds involved in desire.

CHAPTER 4

Hus-Banned: The Worst Foods for Him

As a wife, it's critical to maintain a watch of your husband's diet and stay clear of foods that not only add pounds to his body, but also puts him at danger for significant health problems including heart disease, high blood pressure, and diabetes. Men should eat well, maintain a healthy weight, and exercise regularly as they age, not only to feel better, but also to avoid disease. Men's chances of developing heart disease, high cholesterol, type 2 diabetes, cancer, gout, arthritis, and prostate disorders like BPH increase as they become older. Testosterone levels begin to fall over time, and eating the incorrect foods and/or being overweight can throw hormones off balance. Limiting specific meals is a great way to help men stay healthy by controlling blood sugar, lowering inflammation, and avoiding artery blockage. Certain foods should be avoided in order to avoid disease: It is far easier to prevent disease than it is to treat and manage it once it has occurred.

We all have a basic idea of what food habits to maintain and what lifestyle to live in order to keep our bodies healthy and testosterone levels high. Yes, eating a lot of unhealthy meals can lead to stale workouts, a flabby stomach, and a shortened lifespan. But there's a disastrous consequence lying behind those buckets of finger-licking sweetness that you may not have considered: Your husband's sexual function could be harmed if you eat too much junk food. Keep these things listed below in this chapter, out of the fridge if you want a happy marriage.

Diet soda: Drinking soda on a regular basis is a bad idea, and this includes diet soda. Artificial sweeteners, particularly aspartame, have an immediate impact on your serotonin levels. Serotonin is an important hormone for promoting feelings of well-being and happiness. According to experts, low serotonin levels are linked to reduced libido in both men and women.

Celery: This contains androsterone, a male sex hormone generated through perspiration, which has been found in limited research to boost flirtatious behaviour in females. Ingesting androsterone can also increase male arousal, causing the body to emit smells and signals that make a man more attractive to other women.

Cheap cold cuts: Unlike the plastic wrap you use to wrap leftovers, retail meat and cheese wrappers are frequently made of PVC (polyvinyl chloride), which leaches into fatty foods and causes hormonal disturbances. Due the fact that most of these products such as: red meat, hot dogs, and hamburgers have additional hormones, preservatives, and antibiotics, they can produce a hormonal imbalance in your body, lower-quality meat can contribute to a low-wattage sex drive. To keep your sex drive stimulated, use leaner, unprocessed cuts like chicken or turkey. Have your meat wrapped in brown paper and purchased directly from the butcher.

Licorice: This has to be avoided because it contains Glycyrrhizic acid, the principal ingredient in licorice that gives it its characteristic flavour, can inhibit testosterone production.

Beer: When you consider that a lack of enthusiasm between the sheets could be due to drinking. While all alcohol has an effect on the liver's ability to eliminate excess estrogen, phytoestrogens have a different effect. The hops used to produce beer contain plant-derived estrogens that interfere with the fertility of people who consume them.

CHAPTER 5
Ways To Love Your Husband

What kind of love do you have for your husband? Should you follow a predetermined framework, listen to your mother, or follow your heart? We are born with the ability to love. We don't adore our partner just because someone else tells us to. You must have that emotion from within; you must believe that the man is deserving of your affection. You don't need to look for answers outside once you've reached that level of emotional attachment. Ask yourself, how do I love my husband? and you'll find out. Over time, though, some common characteristics have arisen among women who are madly in love with their spouses. There are various suggestions in this chapter for how to love your partner. If there has been some unpleasantness in the relationship, we also explain how you can try to reintroduce those sentiments. You must learn new ways to love your partner more effectively. You already adore your husband and want to deepen your feelings for him, learn more from the tips listed below.

Take pleasure in your moments: When you make time for each other and know that your love is a priority, your relationship will thrive. Make it a point to spend at least one hour a day together. Make time for him, inquire about his day and tell him about yours, keep him up to date on the gossip, or simply talk about the news. Do something that both of you enjoy, but the most important thing is to spend time together.

Confidence: Have faith in yourself that you are the appropriate companion for your husband and that he loves you more than anyone else. This will give you the guts to not only love but also express your love for your hubby.

Seek his advice: You've received two employment offers. You may be certain about the path to pursue, but don't make a decision without first consulting your husband. Pay attention to what he says because he may have examined the two offers and can provide you with new information. Consider his viewpoint. If you still want to do things your way, talk to him about it and come to an agreement.

Unconditional love: Our hearts are drawn to the one we truly love, when we get a glimpse of that special one. Love should not be based on presents, and it should not be based on external goods. Love isn't a machine that produces output. You can't wait till he buys you a diamond ring or takes you on a romantic trip before you fall in love with him. Because love is an emotion that cannot be controlled, you can lavish him with love regardless of whether or not he meets your expectations.

Activate your passion: Show him what you're capable of doing to make him happy. Your actions will astound him. Make him want more, and make him miss the pleasure when he's not with you. Make the initial move, and see how he reacts to certain situations. And don't just stop there. Tell him what you want and encourage him to be naughty with you so you may have as much fun with sex as he does.

Show that you care: You don't have to wait for him to become ill to show that you care. Wake him up with a cup of coffee in the morning, greet him warmly when he returns home, or offer him a warm massage. All of these actions demonstrate your concern for him.

Put him first: This does not imply that you give up your slice of pizza to him. It implies that you consider him before making a decision or undertaking a task. A basic example would be the daily menu. Consider whether he would prefer broccoli or greens that day before you start cooking. Consider whether your husband would appreciate a dress before purchasing it.

Become his best buddy: If you become his best friend, you won't have to worry about the previous point. When he has anything to say or needs guidance, he knows he can come to you. Gaining his trust, encouraging rather than criticizing him, and being there for him while he is attempting to achieve his goals are all ways to become his buddy.

Display Affection: Let the world know that you love him with a little PDA. Positive things should be said about him, and you should inform your friends and family about his accomplishments and qualities. When you're out with him, don't be afraid to take his hand in yours or to gaze at him and grin. These modest acts will instill confidence in him and make him proud of your devotion.

Listen to him: Allow him to speak, and pay attention to what he has to say. Instead of leaping to conclusions, try to understand his point of view. Even the most vehement disagreements between you can be resolved amicably in this manner.

It's a roller coaster ride: Not all of life's moments are worth laughing about. Every relationship has its ups and downs, and marriage is no exception. You'll have your own set of quarrels, fights, and conflicts. However, you will still be able to love your husband provided you do not become preoccupied with such little concerns. Don't let yourself become hopeless and depressed.

Allow him some privacy: Don't read his texts or listen in on his talks just to see what he's up to. Don't be too interested in finding out who his pals are when he's out with them. He will keep you up to date on events that may directly affect you, as well as talk to you about his friends and career when he has the opportunity. If you suspect him of infidelity or concealment, you may need to make an exception to this rule.

Continue to laugh: Laugh with your friends. Develop a sense of humour, watch some humorous videos, and take pleasure in the moment. There may be things that only you and your partner understand and laugh about. It's important to remember that a couple who laughs together stays together.

CHAPTER 6
How to ignite your spark

You can communicate your love for your hubby through certain gestures. After all, wouldn't you want him to know how much you adore him? When everything is going well in your life, your connection remains solid. When it comes to turbulence, though, the bond is put to the test. Financial, emotional, or physical concerns might cause turbulence. What would you do if he lost his job, cheated on you, or you lost interest in him because you cheated on him? These are all scenarios that can arise in a marriage. This chapter will focus on the greatest ways to rekindle your marriage's romance.

Hug and kiss: Do not wait until bedtime to give him a hug or kiss. Take a few moments here and there to kiss him, hug him when he or you are going out, kiss him when he or you return from work, give him a wicked glance to let him know you are thinking about him, and sleep entwined in his arms. Getting physical with each other will improve your intimacy.

Surprise him with a gift: You don't have to be a recipient all the time; you can also be a provider. Give your husband some practical items. Observe his preferences and determine what he requires. This will assist you in purchasing all of the appropriate items for him. He'll be delighted to accept your gifts.

Play with him: Play a game of cards with him, tennis, or any other game that he enjoys. Work out with him, whether at home or at the gym, if he is a fitness freak. Getting involved in activities that your husband enjoys will bring you closer to him. Your efforts will be much appreciated by him.

Love letters: When was the last time you wrote something for your hubby in the form of a love letter? In the age of WhatsApp, love letters may be a dated concept, but they are still relevant. A lovely, handwritten letter may express your sentiments in a way that no software can.

Do not react: Do not retaliate by arguing when your husband is irritated or has lost his cool. Allow for some time to pass and enable him to chill down. In fact, your silence will bring him back to normal sooner rather than later when he realizes his mistake. After things have calmed down, discuss the situation. This will boost his admiration for you.

Take a few notes from him: In addition to the love lessons, you may ask him to teach you a game or an art form that he excels at. Inquire about learning to drive a car, paint on a canvas, or do a craft from him. The goal is for the two of you to spend some quality time together and admire his abilities.

Dress him up in his favourite clothes: Purchase a handful of his favourites. Inquire about what he wants you to wear, and enlist his assistance in buying for you. You are welcome to wear these clothing when you go out with him. Also, go out and buy some beautiful outfits and surprise him during your private moments. All of these actions show how much you care for him.

CHAPTER 7
SHOWING LOVE IN UNPLEASANT TIMES

A Successful marriage happens when two people grow in love and sustain their commitment with each other. Important persons in your life will face difficulties and sadness from time to time. When a family member, friend, or even a co-worker is going through a difficult time, you'll want to let them know you care. Even if all you can do is offer a small amount of consolation, you want these people to know you're there for them. No matter how new or established your relationship is, you and your girlfriend, fiancée, or wife are bound to have difficult moments together. Through the long term, sticking by the one you care about in difficult circumstances will only strengthen your friendship and establish a strong sense of trust. Don't give up hope, things can be sorted out if you have the desire to rebuild your relationship and still love and care for each other. People are not perfect; they are prone to succumbing to pressure at times. When confronted with these difficult situations, it's easy to want to walk away and forget about the problem. However, it is far better to stay and get therapy for the sake of your relationship and connection.

If someone you care about is going through a difficult period right now, there are certain things you can remind them of that will help them get through it. The most important thing to remember while speaking to someone who is struggling is to make sure your tone of voice and behaviour are acceptable. In a friendly, encouraging manner, remind your loved one of the following things, rather than make chaos from little issues that can be resolved amicably. Your approach will have a significant impact on the answer you receive. The fact that you are attempting to reignite your love shows that you are committed to your relationship. Do not take this to mean that you are making a concession.

Recognize his viewpoint: Consider this scenario: your husband has proposed that you spend a few days with your parents. He may have made the idea with the best of intentions to give you a break, but you may have misinterpreted it as him sending you away to hang out with his buddies. Instead of jumping to conclusions, be mature enough to grasp your husband's perspective.

Take a look at the positive aspects of his personality: You obviously appreciate certain qualities of him because you willingly married him. You must have enjoyed something about him, whether it was his personality, appearance, or behaviour. Take a look at those advantages, and you might find that he isn't as horrible as you imagined.

Return to the past: You may be slipping away from your husband today, but there was a time when you couldn't keep your gaze or your hands away from one other. Consider the occasions in your lives when you and your partner went on romantic vacations, had sensual dates, or simply cuddled up in a quilt at home watching your favourite TV shows. They'll reawaken your feelings, and you might want to reconsider your relationship.

Do not keep grudges against him: Did he fail to fulfil a commitment to take you on a vacation? Is he so unromantic that he never sends you a bouquet of flowers? Don't hold these occurrences against him. Maybe he's not naturally romantic, and he doesn't know how to express his love for you, but he still cares about you. You can forgive tiny disappointments if you are confident in his love and affection for you.

Confront him, but be careful what you say: Being friendly to him does not imply you disregard his wrongdoings. You should address him if you have any doubts about his fidelity or any other misbehaviour. Inquire as to why he chose to be dishonest or wrongful. But first, double-check that your assumptions are correct and that you are not being duped by anyone or anything. Use the appropriate language to communicate to him that you are aware of what he is doing and that you are dissatisfied with it.

Accept him for who he is: No two minds are alike, and you and your husband are no exception. He might forget to hang up his damp towel or turn off the light behind him. You may be a vegetarian, but he refuses to give up his passion for non-vegetarian cuisine. These tiny variances are acceptable because finding a clone for a mate is very difficult.

Control your need to criticize him: Once you begin to appreciate the positive aspects of your husband, you will no longer criticize him. And once you stop critiquing him, you'll be able to appreciate the good in him. Both are inextricably linked. You criticize him in order to have an unfavourable impression of him. The negativity fades away when you resolve to love him again.

CHAPTER 8
Why Love Matters

Love is at the top of nearly everyone's list of characteristics that lead to a good, happy marriage. This says a lot about the power of love and what it can do to keep a relationship together. It's what elevates a decent relationship to greatness, and it's what transforms lovers into closest friends. Love isn't a fool proof solution to all of our relationship's problems. It is far from the final answer to our problems and tribulations in life. This is why it is critical not to exaggerate the power of love and to keep it grounded. While you may believe that "you need love," you also require respect and humility.

Those who have experienced love know how powerful it can be. You might not want to picture your existence without love because it is capable of so much. Regardless, many individuals are curious about the true limits of love. There are times in life when people find themselves in difficult relationships. People in these relationships frequently love their partners deeply, but they often wonder if love is enough to keep things going. The significance of love in marriage is almost limitless. After all, marriage isn't always simple, and without love, you'd never be able to muster the motivation, focus, selflessness, and patience required to make your partnership a long-term success.

Love breeds respect: Respect is the cornerstone of each healthy relationship, and love breeds it. Love and trust cannot grow without respect. You know your comments, thoughts, and feelings are valued when you feel respected. When respect is demonstrated, you are able to trust freely. Emotional support is linked to the value of respect and love in marriage. You are more capable of being vulnerable and confiding in your relationship if they value your thoughts and treat you properly. Emotional support improves mental health, as well as general relationship and self-happiness.

When you're with the one you love, you sleep better: Another facet of love's significance in marriage? Aside from blanket-hogs and snore-hounds, spooning with the love of your life will help you sleep better. Couples who slept next to one another had lower cortisol levels, slept more comfortably, and fell asleep faster than those who slept alone, according to studies.

Sex binds you together: A healthy sexual connection is an important element of married love, not just because it feels fantastic to be so close to your partner, but also because it physiologically links you. Oxytocin, often known as the love drug, is a bonding hormone that is released when you touch your lover and naturally boosts love, self-esteem, feelings of trust, and optimism. The value of love in a marriage is immeasurable. It has health benefits, promotes a tighter link, improves sex life, and decreases daily stress and concerns. You and your spouse won't be able to have a happy, healthy relationship if you don't love each other.

Love makes people happy: Love makes people happy. Whatever you think of being free and independent, there's nothing like the comfort and security of knowing you're being looked after. When you're in love, your body releases dopamine, a neurotransmitter found in the brain's reward area. It's no wonder, then, that dopamine helps you feel valued, pleased, and rewarded, as well as encouraging pleasant feelings. Love also causes a rise in the stress hormone cortisol. While cortisol is generally connected with stress, it is responsible for the butterflies in your stomach, excitement, and intense passion you experience while you are in the throes of new love. Some studies even suggest that your dopamine levels may remain increased as you progress from puppy love to mature love.

Sex strengthens your immune system: Regular sexual activity with your loving partner might enhance your immune system. Compared to their single counterparts, married couples have reduced rates of depression, substance addiction, and blood pressure. People who live alone have a higher risk of heart disease than those who are married.

Love makes you live longer: Couples age more gracefully than singles, and individuals in good marriages enjoy life more than their single counterparts, regardless of age. The emotional, social, and economical support obtained as part of a pair is supposed to impact married couples' long lifespans. Married couples, for example, are more likely to have access to medical care. Once in a committed relationship, married men moderate their lifestyles, such as drinking, fighting, and taking excessive risks.

Sex relieves stress: The value of love in marriage can also be beneficial to your mental health. Loneliness has been shown in studies to be harmful to one's health and to activate pain areas in the brain. Anxiety levels rise as a result of this. Love and sex are fantastic for reducing tension and anxiety. This is aided in part by the production of oxytocin, a bonding hormone. This love drug is responsible for the feelings of attachment you get when you touch someone you care about, whether it's something as intimate as having sex or something as sweet as holding hands. Oxytocin also relieves anxiety and stress by lowering stress levels and balancing neurochemicals.

Enhanced financial stability: Married couples are more likely to be financially secure and accumulate greater money over time than single or divorced partners. Having two incomes provides financial security for couples, which can reduce stress, minimize debt, and allow for marriage flexibility if one partner can only work part-time or prefers to stay at home to care for children or other duties.

CHAPTER 9

Living in Peace with Your Partner

Put your spouse first and serve him or her without reservation. To understand and appreciate each other's opinions, be quick to listen and slow to talk. When we focus our abilities on achieving a single goal, we achieve unity. Our most basic mutual goal in marriage is to love our spouse. In our daily lives, we require guideposts to remind us of our goals.

Discord is not created by a true companion. In the same way that you would not allow anything to come between you and a friend, you should do the same with your spouse. Your friendship will dissolve if you do not keep an eye out for your pal. Friendship is what it is. Friendships exist between husband and wife. As a result, they must run their home as two friends would. Between a husband and a wife, there should be a lot of harmony. It cannot be deemed a husband and wife relationship if there is any hurt in the connection. How can a husband and wife harm each other when even friends do not do so? The highest form of friendship is that which exists between a husband and his wife. Unity is an image of two people who are completely complementary to one another. We can't be together if one partner does all of the talking or has all of the power. We must submit to one another in love, enabling each individual to use their unique gifts to achieve the goals you both want to achieve in any particular season of life. Couples rarely agree on everything, thus the key to success is humble compromise.

Respect: Husbands, put in the effort to demonstrate love. Wives, make an effort to show respect. We all require love and respect, but it is well acknowledged that women place a higher value on love than men do on respect. Focus on demonstrating affection and building a healthy relationship with your wife so she feels safe and cared for. Wives, pay special attention to how you relate to and communicate with your spouse so that he feels appreciated and wanted.

Every day, show compassion to one another: Always be kind to one another in your interactions and in your willingness to help one another. Gratitude for both is appropriate.

Be fast to admit wrongdoing to one another: Do it as soon as you discover the wrong you've done, even if it's minor. Why wouldn't you?

Take as much time as you need to resolve the conflict: It may take some time to work through your areas of tension if you haven't done so already, but it will be worthwhile. Take a break and do something fun that you used to enjoy if it feels like all you do is work through problems. Without mutual delight, a marriage will not thrive. Unresolved conflict robs us of our joy.

Always maintain a sense of humility and forgiveness: A marriage can't thrive without them virtues like humility and forgiveness. When we admit the wrongs we've done to one other, it requires humility and forgiveness to reconnect.

Be Vigilant: Always remember that there is an adversary seeking to destroy your marriage, but that enemy is not your spouse.

Keep in touch: Don't allow resentment drive a distance between you. Either let things go if you truly can, understanding how much your partner endures. Otherwise, talk about any tense or hurt sentiments you're having.

CHAPTER 10

Strategies for Dealing with an Angry Partner

Give your marriage the same amount of thought as you do to your hobbies. People devote a significant amount of time, money, and effort to their hobbies and interests outside of work. When a marriage is making them unhappy, though, some people throw in the towel and conclude it's pointless to try again. Your marriage will benefit from reading books on marriage, conflict resolution, and communication skills. It's even better if you can get your partner to read them.

Treat your spouse with more respect than you would anyone else. Have you ever heard the saying familiarity breeds contempt? People tend to treat their spouses worse than strangers, which is an awful reality. Retrain yourself to treat your spouse with reverence. Separate your interests. Make sure you have some personal space, and make sure your partner has some as well. Marriage necessitates a great deal of closeness, but you don't have to be joined at the hip.

Choose Your Fights and Think Long-Term: The adage choose your battles wisely is applicable not only to military warfare, but also to relationships with enraged partners. Leaders in the military may be willing to lose some battles in order to win the war. They don't usually waste resources and energy on contests that they can't win. Similarly, because people have diverse beliefs, attitudes, interests, and expectations, relationships can be a battleground where practicing moderation is sometimes a good tactic. You may discover a plethora of issues to quarrel with your husband if you want to. However, being judicious and letting go of what means the least will help you. Remember that fighting over every minor disagreement is neither sensible nor realistic. You may win the debate, but your relationship may suffer as a result.

De-escalate and neutralize the situation Emotionality: Trying to control an enraged partner can make them defensive and uncooperative. It is undesirable to become enraged in response to a partner's rage; it is preferable to let the other person to become enraged and accept that they will eventually cool down. The calmer you are, the faster their rage will dissipate. De-ultimate escalation's purpose is to reduce emotional intensity and refocus antagonism toward improved collaboration.

Think Influence, Not Control: Don't try to persuade your partner to change. You can't do it. You can, however, sway your partner by demonstrating the advantages of your perspective. Create a nice environment that encourages cooperation rather than control to influence your partner. When you treat your partner with sweetness, you may draw them closer to you, as well as closer to understanding how and why you feel the way you do. This may improve your chances of achieving positive results. You might be surprised at how much the energy between you and your lover changes and how much your relationship blooms if you use the aforementioned tactics. Many couples could avoid divorce if they received sound counsel and remembered it when their relationship began to falter. Here are a few suggestions that should help most couples.

Act assertively, talk politely: Acting assertively entails assuming a position in which you may express your desires directly and respectfully while also taking into account your partner's feelings and desires. You are confident, honest, and open when you act and speak in an assertively courteous manner. At the same time, being firm encourages your partner to shoulder their portion of the blame.

Think things through: Couples are prone to developing hot button concerns that result in regular squabbles. Waiting before replying to anything that has made you furious can help you avoid bickering. Count to ten with your fingers. It could be better to talk about challenging topics when emotions aren't as high.

Appreciate each other's contributions to the marriage: Marriages frequently collapse due to perceived discrepancies in each party's level of contribution. Try to recognize and value the other person's contributions, whether financial or emotional. Marriage is not an easy task. It takes time, work, and maturity to build a strong marriage. It is, nonetheless, worthwhile.

Reflect on Your Behaviours and Understand the Triggers: Accepting your involvement in being annoyed with an angry partner and reflecting on what actions may provoke their rage is what it means to be responsible. It also entails figuring out what makes you act the way you do. You may become less reactive and more constructive as you grow more conscious. As a result, you, your partner, and your relationship may feel better. If you recognize you contributed to the escalation of a dispute, take responsibility and admit it. Your ownership may help to relieve tension and urge your partner to do the same. People often become enraged because they believe they are not being heard, taken seriously, or acknowledged. Communicate constructively, understand, and validate. They may feel betrayed and unheard. To prevent inflaming your partner's rage, actively listen to them until you are confident that they feel heard and understood. Try to understand their deepest needs and affirm their thoughts and experiences by going beneath the surface. One way we communicate acceptance of ourselves and others is through validation. It does not imply that you agree with everything. Rather, it's about acknowledging and taking into account your partner's point of view. Being present and sincerely attempting to comprehend is the key to validation. It means paying attention to both your partner and your personal experience, rather than pushing it away or avoiding it.

When Your Partner Is Calm, Address Your Problem: When your partner's emotional state is elevated, their cognitive abilities may be compromised. It's pointless to address your problem as long as the rage reigns supreme. Allow time for the negative energy to dissipate before engaging in a more sensible conversation. Address the topic that caused your partner's rage when you're both cool and collected. They may be more receptive to hearing and understanding during this time. Remember to apply this guideline to yourself as well. Take time to relax yourself when you're emotional or angry portions are active. Anger feeds on itself, while relaxing produces a more peaceful environment.

Be your spouse's partner: Keep each other up to date on your daily activities, including your work days and what you do at home. Every day, the time you spend alone outside in the world is really important. At the conclusion of the day, always talk to each other about how your day went.

Don't give up: Marriages wax and wane, as every married person will tell you. There are excellent, bad, and mediocre times in life. If the good overcomes the bad by a small margin, a marriage is viable. The simpler it gets, and the more warmth and connection you have for your spouse, the more you cherish the good and try to let the bad go.

Encourage your partner's ambitions and dreams: In a happy marriage, one spouse is pleased with the accomplishments of the other. Good spouses encourage each other to achieve their goals. Goals, such as a career shift, can be frightening at times and require careful consideration. Collaborate on the project.

Do not believe that the grass is always greener on the other side: Most people who leave their marriages for someone else face the same issues in their new relationship, and many regret not working things out in their first marriage.

Practice Patience and Compassion: Anger often masks deeper and more vulnerable emotions like fear, grief, or suffering, which your spouse may find more difficult to discuss. Anger acts as a protective shield for a short time, making your partner feel powerful and in command. In the end, however, it damages them from within. This is why it's critical to show compassion to your partner and refrain from blaming or accusing them.

Be Calm: Patience can be used as an antidote to your own and your partner's wrath. It includes exercising wisdom when rage develops. It's all about waiting not speaking or acting in an automatic or reactionary manner. Patience and compassion are the bedrocks of good energy and human interaction.

Find activities that you and your spouse like doing together: Marriage is a partnership. If you and your partner have completely different hobbies, you will gradually drift away. Find common interests, pursuits, and pleasures, but keeping in mind that these activities will most likely vary over time.

Forgive each other: Marriage is a long commitment, and awful things will inevitably happen. Every couple makes mistakes and mistreats each other from time to time. You must be able to forgive and move on from your spouse's wrongdoings. Remember that the next time you need forgiveness, it may be you.

Always assume the best in your partner: Everyone has miscommunications and misunderstandings. If your spouse's activities irritate you, wait a while and then try to figure out why. You may discover that your spouse intended to be constructive rather than negative, and that you misinterpreted or assumed.

Don't sweat the small stuff: Prioritization is crucial, just as it is in the workplace. Choose your battles carefully, and let the rest go.

Give your spouse a treat now and then: If your spouse like something, provide it without being asked, even if you don't like it. It could be something as simple as a movie date, a ride to a favourite destination for your spouse, or even a favourite grocery store treat.

Compliment your spouse at least once a day: This promotes a healthy relationship and is the correct thing to do, as your spouse is likely doing a lot of excellent things every day.

Don't squabble with your partner over the kids: Children's disagreements can be quite damaging to a marriage. Have your disagreements off-line so your kids don't know you're arguing. If necessary, seek professional advice to assist you in coordinating and respecting your many points of view.

Be dependable: Many marriages are destroyed by affairs. If you can't stop yourself from falling in love with someone outside of your marriage, be honest with everyone and end the marriage first.

Grow Together: To build financial stability with your spouse, work together: The formation of a solid economic joint venture is one of the advantages of marriage. It will be one of the things that makes you feel good about each other and the world as your financial security grows. It will also be a reflection of how well you and your spouse have worked together during your marriage.

Don't tell your friends and family about your issues: One complaint spoken during a difficult period in your marriage will reverberate with the listener long after the issue or squabble has been settled. Find an unbiased professional to talk to about your marriage if you need to.

Spend time with mutual friends: It is generally beneficial for a marriage to pursue outside friendships jointly, whether with single people or other couples.

CHAPTER 11
Happily Married Forever

Everyone wishes to be happy, yet happiness is a fleeting emotion. When life pushes happiness away, successful couples learn to purposefully do things that will bring it back. Long-term marriages go through periods when you get along well at times and don't at others. It's absurd to expect to feel connected and happy in your relationship all of the time. People change, circumstances change, and as a result, marriages last when people are adaptable and find new methods to deal with new conditions.

Communicate: We're just exhausted a lot of the time. Heart-to-heart conversations are becoming increasingly rare. When we hold on to our resentment, anger, or hurt, however, it festers and slowly poisons a connection. To keep the lines of communication open, you must communicate with one another. To set aside time to chat and truly listen to one another. Take the time to communicate frequently and to listen when you do. You're part of a group, and a group can only function at its best when everyone on the team is on the same page.

Make your partner laugh: Be wacky, silly, and quirky as often as you can to make your companion laugh. When you're married, some of the best nights aren't out on the town or at a beautiful dinner. Instead, it's those fleeting times when you're just the two of you, giggling and fooling about.

Make your family your first priority: Love comes first, then marriage, then careers, children, bills, and stress. When managing employment, children, and finances, it's easy to lose sight of the people for whom you're doing it all. They are always there, after all, and this opportunity or expense is just temporary. It's possible that if you lose sight of your loved ones, they won't always be there. Especially if the people you care about start to feel like a secondary consideration rather than the driving force behind your every decision. Ensure that your family remains your top priority, and that they are aware of this. Remind them as much as you can.

Don't do anything that can jeopardize the relationship: This isn't only about infidelity. This is about not keeping crucial information from your partner hidden. Don't pretend to be working late when you actually went to the bar with some employees. They were smitten by you and put their faith in you. Do your partner a favour by being open and honest about the things that matter to them.

Stay Active: Keep the romance alive by resisting the urge to fall into a routine. Your enthusiasm has no bounds in the beginning.

There's a lot of spontaneity here, as well as a lot of fun and playful fantasy. Over time, however, we become preoccupied with job, children, and household tasks, and we become too weary, anxious, and preoccupied to see that we have forgotten about intimacy as a part of our lives. Date dates are fun, but don't forget how much you both loved those spontaneous times. No, it isn't simple, especially when children are involved. But it's not difficult to chisel out a few moments here and there to regain that spark and keep the fires ablaze.

Don't be scared to take time apart to do your own thing: You adore each other, and you probably wanted to spend every minute with each other at first. That's quite typical. You'll need to learn to be okay with doing your own thing now and then as time goes on. Getting out of the house and leaving the children and housekeeping with your spouse might be a terrific way to strengthen your marriage. Just make sure you both have that chance.

Honesty: Little white lies aren't that bad; honesty is crucial. It is a necessary component of any happy relationship. However, there are occasions when it is preferable to utter a small white lie rather than say nothing at all. The idea here is to tread carefully. Your partner's faith in you as the one person who will tell them the truth when it matters should never waver. However, if they adore a new wardrobe or hairstyle and you aren't convinced, tell them the truth. When it comes to something significant, something that will break their heart or expose them to ridicule, be honest. However, if they adore their fuzzy pink socks and you think they're terrible, let them keep them and be blissfully unaware that you think they're hideous.

Find out what makes your lover happy: It's not only about the great jesters. It's all about the little things. The odd little things your lover enjoys. Once you've figured out what they want, make sure you give it to them as often as you can. This demonstrates that you are paying attention and are concerned about their happiness. That they and their happiness are your top priorities.

Be Faultless: It doesn't matter who began it or who is right or wrong; be the first to apologize. You probably uttered some things you shouldn't have, things you didn't mean, in the heat of the fight. Fighting takes two people, and making up takes two people. Don't waste time waiting for the apology you believe you deserve. Instead, be the first to say "I'm sorry." After you've apologized, you're more likely to receive an apology in return and for your spouse to listen to your side of the story.

Get over your jealousy: In today's world, males collaborate with women. Women collaborate with males. We are more likely to have friends of the opposing sex than we are to have friends of the same sex. You married your lover. And that matters a lot more than we realize sometimes. Trust your spouse not to hurt your heart, to make the best decisions, and to be honest with you about any scenario that may happen. Because you married them, you can be confident that they are deserving of your trust. Make sure you're making the proper decisions and communicating with your partner.

Compliment generously: When you first started dating, you told your partner everything you liked about them. You never hesitated to tell them they looked fantastic, smelled great, or that they are brilliant, witty, and all-around amazing. We tend to forget about those things after we get married. On our worst days, when the kids have worn us down or our work has grinded us to a halt, the one thing that may lift us up the most is hearing those same words from someone who truly cares about us. Never stop reminding the person you care about how wonderful they are, how amazed you are by them, and how you will never lose faith in them.

Never blame your partner: If something goes wrong, don't blame your partner. Do not make your debates a competition. If somebody said something hurtful and you responded with something hurtful. They are in charge of what they have spoken. You, on the other hand, are responsible for what you say. You are in charge of your emotions, feelings, and actions. In the end, both sides are responsible for a portion of the blame. Concentrate on identifying and accepting responsibility for your part, as well as apologizing for it.

CONCLUSION

In short, keep track of all the reasons you're in love. Never forget to tell your partner how much you still care for them and why. When the world breaks them down, remind them that you're here to help them get back on their feet and that you believe in them.

Be considerate: Do for your partner what you would have them do for you. Think about how your words and actions will affect others. Consider how you'd like to be spoken to, treated, and cared for. Then go ahead and accomplish those things.

Have a good time: Laugh at each other and don't take yourself too seriously. Don't try to be funny by putting your partner down, being belittling, or insulting them; this isn't cool and will get you in trouble. Couples who play together are more likely to stay together. Make it a point to undertake an enjoyable activity with your partner on a regular basis to maintain a great relationship.

Give it your all: Marriage is a limitless possibility. Your time is one of the most valuable things you can give. Love with all of your senses: your heart, head, and soul.

Don't try to alter your spouse: Many couples get into difficulties because they believe that once they get married or even in a committed relationship, they must transform their partner into their ideal mate. We must keep in mind that we will never be all-rounders.

You're a team, and you're unstoppable when you work together.